Wire Jewellery Manual

Icon jewelleryUK

All you need to know aout tools wires
polishing and much more.....

David Morris

About the Author:

I have been a wire worker and jewellery maker for over 20 years.

I live in Cardiff the capital city of Wales in the United Kingdom.

I have sold my own wire jewellery online also on my own stall in a market in the city.

Over the years I have amassed a large number of tools and quite a bit of knowledge about wire jewellery

Both making and selling.

This e book is mainly for the beginner but I am sure there are things here for the more experienced wireworker too.

I wish you well on your journey into wire jewellery making.

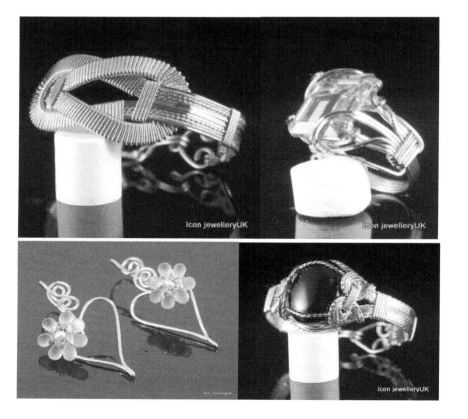

Very few tools are needed to make wire jewellery.

You may think that is a bold statement, yet it is true. It is possible to make beautiful wire jewellery with just four tools.

These basic tools are very surprising in their simplicity.

Wire jewellery making basically consists of using tools to bend, curl and wrap wires around themselves and then setting beads, cabochons and facetted stones into various harnesses that you make out of the wires.

You can easily make the harnesses using only the following four tools.

1. Flat nose or Square nose jewellery maker's pliers.
2. Round nose jewellery maker's pliers.
3. Chain nose jewellery maker's pliers.
4. Jewellery maker's Flush cutters.

JEWELLERY MAKER'S PLIERS.

All the pliers are jewellery making pliers and they must have smooth jaws, not serrated or ridged like general household or electrical pliers.

You don't want the ridges inside the jaws of the pliers because they will mark the wire when you use them.

Jewellery making tools are usually slightly smaller and lighter than general household tools and the average size is about 5 ½ inches in length. It is possible to find them up to 6½ inches if you are a male with larger hands.

The important thing is to buy tools in a size that you are comfortable using. After all they are going to become very important to you, the very things that you are going to be creating with, and they must be right for you.

The great thing about wire jewellery making is that it need not be an expensive hobby.

Pliers are available from the very cheap Chinese imported tools to the very expensive Lindstrom jewellery making pliers that can cost up to £30 plus, per pair. I would recommend that those who are just beginning should start with the lower priced tools and as you gain experience upgrade your tools accordingly.

FLAT NOSE OR SQUARE NOSE PLIERS.

The main use is for bending wires to angles and to flatten or squeeze wires down to hold them securely.

These are the pliers that you will use to make what are called "wraps" around bundles of wires to hold them together. Also used to form flat spirals.

ROUND NOSE OR ROSARY PLIERS.

Round nosed pliers are used to form looping movements and to make hooks and eyes for catches on bracelets and necklaces.

Round nosed pliers can have a graduated jaw or a stepped jaw usually about 1 inch in length. The most common are graduated and for basic purposes these will be the pliers to choose when beginning wire jewellery making.

CHAIN/SNIPE NOSE PLIERS.

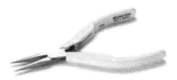

Chain nose pliers are similar to flat nose pliers except that the jaws are usually tapered to thin small tip.

They are extremely useful for using in tight areas where normal flat nose pliers cannot reach. They are also available in a "bent nose" version where the tips are angled to allow you to get even further into small places.

FLUSH CUTTERS.

Flush cutters are so named because they are intended to snip the end of a thin piece of jewelry wire, leaving it even, or flush. They range in size and design but all share the same intent -- to provide the jewellery maker with a smooth surface on the wire so it can then be shaped or soldered. Other types of cutters may leave an angled or ragged end on the wire that has been cut. To accomplish a smooth cut, flush cutters have finer, sharper edges that help them avoid leaving a ridge on the wire, sometimes called a pinch .

With these four tools you can perform almost every move that is required to make beautiful wire wrapped and wire sculpted jewellery.

Like all tools these tools are very robust but you must take care not to nick or mark the jaws as this will leave marks on the soft wires you will be using, so a rack or tool holder to store your tools on when you are not using them is much better than having them lying around on your bench where they can bang together and get damaged.

There are of course many more tools out there that you will help you as you progress and move on to more advanced wire work.

There follows a longer list of the tools available and a basic explanation of their uses.

CHAPTER TWO WIRE WORKING TOOLS
(Advanced).

BAIL MAKING PLIERS.

These pliers come in various sizes depending upon the size of the bail you are making.

They usually have jaws of different diameters, such as 3.5mm + 5.5mm or 6mm + 8.5mm etc.

With these pliers you can make bails on pendants and create loops of various sizes.

STEPPED JAW PLIERS.

Similar to bail pliers and used for mostly the same things stepped jaw pliers give you several different sized steps on the jaws of the pliers. Again can be used for making loops and creating bails on pendants.

NYLON JAW PLIERS.

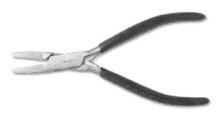

Nylon jaw pliers are very useful to wire workers.

They are particularly useful for straightening wires without marking them. Also they can be used for hardening wire. They can be used for holding your work without marking it.

SPECIALIST PRONG PLIERS

If you progress onto making prong set wire rings then you will need these specialist pliers for forming the prongs for the stone setting.

The size of the prongs changes with the size and shape of the stone you are setting into the ring shank.

Typical sizes available are: 1mm 1.5mm and 2mm.

MANDRELS.

As you progress in wire jewellery making, you may wish to make wire rings and bracelets.

In order to do that you will need to buy yourself mandrels to shape the rings and bracelets on. They come in several types. Some are plain and some ring mandrels are marked with ring sizes on them.

The cheapest most basic ring mandrels are made from hard plastic, really only useful for measuring rings. Then come lightweight aluminium, again these are very light and not really up to the heavy treatment needed to from rings and bracelets.

Next we have wooden ring mandrels. These are perfectly good for forming rings and as long as you are not too rough with them they will do the job.

Steel mandrels are of course the best, they will take any amount of bashing with a rawhide mallet to form the rings and bracelets and if you can afford them these are the ones to purchase as they will last a lifetime.

Ring mandrels are of course round, but you can purchase square, triangular and oval mandrels too.

Black plastic ring mandrel   Aluminium ring mandrel   Hardwood ring mandrel   Steel ring mandrel

A ring mandrel with the sizes marked on it (make sure you purchase one with the ring sizes that correspond to your counties ring size code) is particularly useful. If you cannot get one with the sizes already marked on it like the ones above, you can easily buy a set of ring sizers and use a sharpie marker to mark the mandrel at the size you need for sizing your ring.

Most of the ring mandrels on the market are marked with American sizes but you can easily convert them to Euro/English sizes with a conversion chart found in the back of this booklet.

BRACELET MANDRELS.

Just like ring mandrels bracelet mandrels come in plastic, wood, aluminium and steel. They are usually smooth with no markings. You can get graduated ones or stepped ones and they also come in either a round or an oval shape.

They are used for shaping bracelets to fit the shape of the wrist or arm.

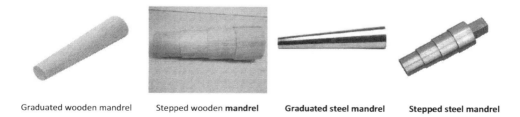

Graduated wooden mandrel   Stepped wooden **mandrel**   **Graduated steel mandrel**   **Stepped steel mandrel**

Neck mandrels are used to form wire collars to the shape of a neck. They are usually made from steel.

Steel neck mandrel   Sterling silver wire collar formed on a neck mandrel

PIN VISE

A pin vise is a hand held powered drill used for drilling very small holes. However wire workers use them for twisting small lengths of square wire to form what we call filigree wire.

Instead of inserting a drill bit into the open jaws of the vise we insert square wire then we tighten the jaws and twist the vise to twist the square wire.

Steel Pin vise

Battery operated wire twister:

When you begin to make larger items like wide band bracelets and neck collars you will want to twist longer lengths of wire.

Whilst this is possible using a pin vise to twist about an inch at a time, twisting several 12 inch lengths is a time consuming job.

For big jobs like this it's time to break out the auto wire twister.

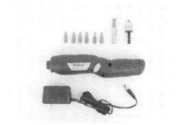

Battery operated screwdriver/wire twister.

What you need is a **battery operated** or **low power** screwdriver with a 3 pronged chuck head attachment.

DO NOT USE AN ELECTRIC DRILL!

They are far too powerful and will not only break the wire they are potentially very dangerous to use in this way.

Insert your SQUARE wire into the chuck head, hold the other end of the wire in a pair of flat nosed pliers. Twist the wire to the desired amount of even twists.
This only takes a few seconds to do and gives a fine even twist to the wire. Be careful not to over twist the wire as it will break if taken too far.

Twisted wire gives a pleasing filigree effect to the wire and adds sparkle to your wire jewellery.

MALLETS AND HAMMERS.

RAWHIDE MALLET

Most wire workers will have what is known as a "Rawhide mallet" made from dried untanned leather rolled into a cylinder and attached to a straight wooden handle. It is used for flattening and forming metals.

Rawhide mallet

NYLON HEAD MALLET/HAMMER

Used for the same purposes as a rawhide mallet these nylon headed mallets are long lasting and tough yet gentle enough not to mark your wire.

Nylon headed mallet/hammer

Mallets and hammers are used by wire workers to form and shape rings, bracelets and neck collars by gently tapping them whilst on, or wrapped around, a mandrel. The action of hammering the wire/metal will not only form it but it will also harden it considerably.

Again used for shaping and forming metals. Wire name writers use them for flattening out edges of letters when they are forming script writing in wire. Usually used with metal stakes or small anvils.

Planishing hammer

SAFETY GLASSES AND HEAD MAGNIFIERS

It is recommended when working with wire that you wear some kind of safety glasses. This is most important when cutting the ends off wires as they can fly off at all kinds of angles.

Safety glasses

HEAD MAGNIFIERS

Head magnifiers come in many styles some with lights attached and interchangeable lenses. Others don't have lights and have magnifying loupe like eye attachments. Because you will be doing close work for long periods of time it makes sense to use a magnifier so that you don't strain your eyes.
Also you will be making small items that you need to see clearly so that you do not snip off the wrong wire by mistake.

Head magnifier with a light and changeable lenses

Types of Wire.

GOLD WIRE:

Gold wire comes in various purities or karats.

**24kt = 99.9% purity. 18kt =
75% purity
14kt = 58.3% purity 12kt =
50% purity**

9kt = 37.5% purity

Because pure gold is too soft for making wire jewellery it is often made into an alloy using other common metals.

Usually copper and or silver that make up the rest of the alloy to 100%. Gold does not tarnish, rust, or corrode and has great strength. It is the most malleable of all the metals. A single ounce of gold can be drawn through a plate into a wire shape that is incredibly thin and incredibly long.

Gold doesn't only come in a yellow colour. It also comes in:

Red gold, Rose gold and Pink gold: This has copper added to give the red colour. The more copper the deeper the colour achieved.

White gold: White gold can have palladium or platinum added to it to give it the white colour. Sometimes nickel is added but this can cause an allergic reaction in people and is not a popular choice.

Green gold: Green gold is given its colour by the addition of silver to the gold and copper alloy

In the present market gold is very expensive and its use in wire jewellery is now limited by that high cost.

SILVER WIRE:

Fine silver: 99.9% pure. It has very little added if anything and is very soft. Because of that it is often used in wire knitting projects.

Sterling silver: Sterling is 92.5% percent pure plus it has 7.5% other metals usually copper mixed in. Copper makes silver harder but it also encourages the silver to tarnish. Tarnish occurs when the silver reacts with gasses in the air or other objects it

comes into contact with. It has more tensile strength and is a little stiffer to work with than pure silver. Silver has been used in jewellery for thousands of years but since the 16th Century more silver has been mined than ever before. Sterling is the most commonly used silver wire in wire jewellery making at this time.

Argentium silver: Argentium silver like sterling has a silver content of 92.5%.

The remaining 7.5% consists of a rare metal called Germanium. It is that metal that gives Argentium its non- tarnishing properties. It is also why Argentium is more expensive than sterling silver. Argentium is now becoming very popular amongst wire jewellery makers for its non-tarnish properties.

GOLD FILLED WIRE:

Gold Filled wire is extremely popular amongst wire jewellery makers and is only now slowing down because of the high cost of gold that prohibits most amateur wire

jewellery makers from purchasing it. Gold filled wire is made by bonding a layer of gold to a layer of base metal usually jewellers brass. It is then either rolled into plate or drawn through a draw plate to form a wire.

Gold filled products must be a minimum of 1/20th by weight of the total piece if it is true gold filled. It is labelled according to the karat of the gold used:

1/20th 10kt gf
1/20 12kt gf
1/20th 14kt gf

Gold filled products can and often do last a lifetime and longer. It is not unusual to find gold filled pieces that are over a hundred years old in very good condition. Gold filled has been referred to as the "Gold of the future" because it offers all the same physical characteristics as solid gold such as, beauty, durability, and strength but at a fraction of the cost. Since the gold is on the outer surface area it is nearly impossible to tell the difference between solid gold and gold filled, except when it comes to the cost.

IMITATION GOLD WIRE:

Dix gold
Yellow brass
High brass
Nu gold
Merlins gold

All the above wires are nearly all made up from the same ingredients. 70% copper and 30% zinc. They do not normally contain Lead or Nickel. They are not long lasting and will wear with time; they will tarnish eventually and loose their bright shine.

They are however, being used more now due to the current economic climate and their affordability. It is the copper that gives them their gold look-alike properties. They are generally soft and easy to work with.

Gold plated: Generally in jewellery making gold is plated onto copper over a base layer of nickel, it is this nickel that often causes the bad reactions to people's skin who wear plated jewellery. Unlike gold filled, **gold plated** has very little gold content at all. In most cases it is only a few microns in thickness. Both copper and silver will migrate or diffuse into the gold layer and that causes a gradual fading of the gold colour and eventually bad tarnishing will occur.

IMITATION SILVER WIRES:

Alpaca silver
German silver
Pakton
New silver
Nickel silver
White brass (sometimes used as an imitation silver)

All the above wires are used as substitutes for silver but are in fact imitation silver.
They are all much the same in their content; 65% copper, 18% nickel and 17% zinc. Sometimes they may have tin and antimony. These wires are now becoming more popular because of the rising costs of the precious metal wires.

BRONZE WIRE:

Bronze wire
Red brass
Low brass
Nu gold
Merlins gold

True **bronze wire** is brittle and hard to work. Bronze wires are usually an imitation bronze based on the colour alone. It has a high copper content: 85% copper and 15% zinc and that is what gives it a deep golden colour. All the above can be seen advertised as bronze wire.

BRASS WIRE:

Brass wire
High Brass
Low Brass
Yellow brass
Red brass
White brass
Jewellers brass

All the above are forms of the same wire with higher or lower levels of copper and zinc content to give the brass wire different properties. Brass wire can be bought in soft or hard forms and both are used in the wire jewellery making trade. Brass

wire was once considered more of a practice wire but is now being used as a metal worthy of sale in its own right. It is a great substitute for gold filled as the economy keeps driving up the price of gold.

ALUMINIUM WIRE:
Aluminium wire in its pure form is very soft so it is usually alloyed with copper, zinc and magnesium to give it added stiffness. In jewellery making it is usually anodised aluminium that is

used. Anodised aluminium is created by dipping the aluminium in a sulphuric acid solution and passing an electric current through it. The surface of the metal reacts with oxygen to produce a thin layer of aluminium oxide. This layer won't flake or peel and is resistant to scratches. It does accept dyes readily and this is how we get the bright attractive colours used in coloured aluminium wire in jewellery making.

COPPER WIRE:

Copper Wire in its pure state is very soft and as it is drawn through the draw plates to form the wire it becomes more and more hard or brittle. It is usually then annealed by placing it in a furnace and heating it up till it returns to its soft state. Cooper wire for jewellery making is usually very soft and buttery and easy to work with. It does not however have very good strength and will distort under pressure. Cooper wire is now available in shapes as well as the round. It is being used more and more by the wire sculpted community where half round and square wires are very popular.

Enamelled copper wire: Enamelled copper wire comes in many bright colours and is very popular amongst jewellery makers. The enamel is sprayed onto the wire but it can be scratched with tools and will eventually wear off with use. The enamelled wire
is generally only available in round shapes.

NIOBIUM WIRE:

Niobium is a member of a small family of metals known as refractory metals.   All the colour you see on the niobium wire is refracted light, no dyes, colourings or paints are used. The amount of oxide determines the colour you see. Electrochemical oxidisation processes are used to create the colour. Niobium is hypo-allergenic, it is frequently used in artificial joints, plates, pacemakers and dental implants. It is the safest metal body.you can wear and is safe to be used for ear wires or for jewellery that penetrates the

WIRE TEMPERS

The temper of wire denotes the hardness or softness of the wire along with the ability fro it to bend fluidly and to hold its shape. Wire temper can range from dead soft to spring hard.

Dead soft: Common in wire sculpted jewellery making it is usually used to make soft flowing curls and swirls to decorate your pieces. It is easy on your fingers and hands and when forming this wire you will usually just use your hands and no tools. Dead soft wire is very forgiving and you may be able to undo mistakes in some cases. Bending dead soft wire will make it harder, this is commonly known as "work hardening". Drawing the wire through a cloth repeatedly or through a pair of nylon jaw pliers will also harden dead soft wire. Some disadvantages of dead soft wire are, it can feel flimsy, shapes will distort very easily if pressure is applied. Tools will leave marks if care is not used.

¼ **hard:** Slightly harder than dead soft wire it will hold its shape slightly more. This temper of wire is hard to find and is not really used much in wire jewellery making, most people moving on to the next level where more control is available.

½ **hard:** This wire is much firmer than both dead soft and ¼ hard wire and it will hold its shape far more readily. However it is harder to work with and it will work harden very quickly. It is not really suitable for making curls and swirls. Commonly used when making wire ring shanks, bracelet harnesses, catches, hooks, etc and also for making the rings used in chain maille jewellery.

Full hard/Spring hard: This wire springs back to its natural shape. Mostly used for making the pins/springs for brooches in wire jewellery making.

Memory wire: Similar to the spring hard wire above this wire returns to its original state but it is usually available only in tight coils and is used mostly by beaders to make beaded bracelets and rings.

WIRE SHAPES AND THEIR USES

Round: Round wire in jewellery making is very common and very ancient and is used in many different ways. Typically in modern times it is used for wire wrapping styles. Seen a lot in wire wrapped freeform cabochons and for wire wrapped beads used to make necklaces, bracelets and rosaries. Smaller gauges of round wire are also used for making ear wires. In its thicker gauges it is used to make clasps, and hooks along with various findings for jewellery making.

Half round: Half round wire is generally used along with other wires as a means of binding together bundles of wires in the process of making wire jewellery.

Square: Square wire is used mostly in wire sculpting or wrapping as the square profile of this wire makes it easier to lay wires next to one another and have them stay in order. Square wire also gives a pleasing sleek look / finish to the jewellery pieces. Square wire can also be twisted to give a filigree wire that when added to jewellery gives a Victorian look.

Triangle: Triangular wire is rare and hard to find and is seldom used in wire jewellery making.

Flat: Flat wire is generally used by both silver and goldsmiths to form bezels for both cabochon and stone settings. It can also be used in wire jewellery making for ring shanks and bracelet harnesses.

Pattern flat wire: As in flat wire it can be used for all the same purposes. It does come in many degrees of thickness, widths and patterns.

Gallery wire: The difference between gallery wire and pattern wire is that gallery wire is generally pierced or filigree in design

This by no means the definitive list of **wires** and their uses. It is more a list of the wires that I have come across and learned about during my time as a wire jewellery maker and designer. I am certain that there are many more wires out there waiting to be discovered so please do keep looking and learning all about wires and their uses in wire jewellery making.

CHAPTER FOUR.
TUMBLING YOUR JEWELLERY

There are many different types of tumblers available to wire jewellery makers. The most common and the one used by most is the "Rotary Tumbler" type.

You want your tumbler to have a strong rubber barrel and a good powerful motor that can tumble the weight of your shot, liquid and jewellery without burning out.

Loritone tumblers are very popular amongst wire jewellery makers.
If you have a lot of jewellery to tumble at the same time you can purchase a doublebarrelled model.

Single barrel tumbler   Double barrel tumbler

TYPES OF SHOT

Stainless Steel Shot – Slightly more expensive Stainless steel shot is easier to use as it will not rust.

Steel Shot – Ordinary steel shot will do the job but you have to dry it after every use or it will rust if not kept completely dry.

Steel Tumbling Media – Shapes:

Round Steel Balls – good all round media for getting a great surface polish

Steel Cones – Works well on curved surfaces like bracelets and other designs

Oval Steel Balls – Provides more surface contact than round balls
Ball-cones – Combines the polishing ability of round balls and the ability of cones to reach into corners and recesses.

Pins – Tapers – Pointed ends can reach into narrow and hard to reach places and between wires. Best used with other shapes so don't use them alone. This is the most likely shape to find stuck in your piece of jewellery when you are finished tumbling, so be sure to carefully examine your jewellery after tumbling to make sure that there is no shot lodged in the wire. If you find a piece of shot in between wires, it can easily be removed, use care not to damage your jewellery.

Eclipse Balls – Round balls that have slightly flattened ends. They are cheaper, and will do a lot of the work previously mentioned.

Jeweller's Mix - This blends several types and sizes of the shot, and is the most popular mix for most jewellery makers. It does a great job. It is my first choice and the shot that I use myself. It gets into all the hidden places as well as doing an excellent job of polishing the jewellery to a professional finish.

WHAT CAN YOU TUMBLE POLISH IN A ROTARY TUMBLER

Once, rotary tumblers were the domain of the rockhound and lapidary artists to polish rocks and gems, but now many wire jewellery artists are using them to polish and harden their wire jewelry. You can polish most jewelry items in your tumbler that contain...

GEMSTONES CABOCHONS
GEMSTONE CARVINGS SILVER AND
GOLD WIRE
BRASS, COPPER, AND NICKEL WIRE

However there are certain items that you should be very wary of polishing in your tumbler

PEARLS - tumble with caution
CAMEOS - tumble with caution
DYED CORALS - tumble with caution
TURQUOISE - tumble with caution
FOIL BACK SWAROVSKI - do not tumble
GEMSTONE DRUSY - do not tumble
OPAL - do not tumble
MALACHITE – do not tumble

NON TARNISHING COPPER OR BRASS WIRE - do not tumble
ARGENTIUM ANTI TARNISH STERLING SILVER WIRE - tumble with caution.

Only tumble Argentium silver wire with extreme caution. It can discolor in a tumbler, it may not always happen but it is always a possibility. Be sure your tumbler barrel is very clean if you are going to try it, and it you can only tumble Argentium only in that barrel, use another barrel for your other metals.

Never tumble coated wire, such as non-tarnish brass and copper wires, the coating will wear off and they should not need tumbling anyway.

Your tumbler is a fantastic tool, you won't believe how shiny and bright it will make your handcrafted jewellery.

Recently wire jewellery artists are using tumblers more and more to polish and harden their jewellery

Tumbling your jewellery will bring a high polish to your artwork and also workharden the piece so it is more durable, and it often removes small nicks and scratches and tool-marks. Work-hardening your jewelry will make an heirloom quality, long lasting and durable piece of jewelry.

GETTING STARTED WITH YOUR TUMBLER.

You'll need:

A tumbler and the steel shot of your choice

Blue original Dawn dish detergent or a burnishing compound that you can buy as a powder that you mix with water or you can purchase it already made up into a liquid.

A wire strainer

Some Paper towels or a cloth towel.

1. Open the rubber canister by removing the nut, washer, metal lid and the innerrubber lid. If you have difficulty removing the outer metal lid use a spoon or the metal washer as a lever to carefully pry to lid loose.

2. Carefully pour all of the steel shot into the empty canister. Be careful not to loseany shot while you do this. For a 3 lb barrel, you'll want to use a pound of shot.

3. Add the items you want to tumble. You can usually fit up to six average size piecesin a 3lb barrel at one time.

4. Pour enough water into the canister to just cover the shot and the jewelry,approximately an inch of water over the level of the shot and jewellery. Use distilled water to ensure there are no contaminants in the water, but that's optional.

5. Add two drops of Original Blue Dawn Dish Detergent (recommended) or theequivalent. DO NOT USE ANY CITRUS BASED DETERGENT! And don't add more than a couple drops or it might foam too much and leak out of the barrel.

6. Insert the inner rubber seal lid and make sure it is tightly sealed against theshoulder of the barrel.

7. Place the metal lid over barrel and then place the washer over the screw, place thenut on the screw and turn until snug. Do not over-tighten the nut or use any tool to tighten the nut, over-tightening could cause the lid to warp and leak.

8. Place the barrel onto the tumbler frame and turn on the switch (or plug it in,depending if your model has a switch).

9. Let run undisturbed for desired length of time. Remember not to tumble GoldFilled items for more than 2 two hours. Two hours will generally get most items bright and shiny unless they are very tarnished, in which case they may take longer.

10. Stop the tumbler, remove the barrel and carefully unscrew the lid and remove thenut and washer.

11. Remove the metal lid. Often it is difficult to pry off with just your hands, you canuse a spoon or the metal washer as a lever to carefully pry the lid off. Insert the edge of the spoon or washer carefully into the space around the edge of the lid and twist slightly to one side to loosen the lid.

12. Have your mesh strainer handy and carefully remove the inner rubber lid,carefully pour the contents of the barrel into the strainer (over a sink or container). Watch out that you don't lose any shot, especially down the drain. Again, you might want to use a mesh sink-drain-strainer set in the drain to catch anything if it falls.

13. Rinse the contents of the strainer under the faucet to rinse off any soap residue,still being careful to not drop anything down the drain.

14. Pour the contents of the strainer onto a towel or paper towels

15. Let the shot dry, rinse out the barrel and lids and dry everything thoroughly.Before storing everything, make sure the shot is completely dry, especially if it is carbon steel and not stainless, it will rust.

Now you should have a beautiful professional finish on your jewelry.

Other tips:

If you are going to be tumbling chains it makes sense not to tumble more than one chain at a time, more than one will tangle together and you will have to spend a lot of time untangling the chains.

You can use other dish washing liquids than Dawn, just don't use anything with citrus or other perfumes, it can discolour the metal.

Some people add a small amount of burnishing compound instead of Dawn.

Be very cautious if you decide to tumble plated or coated metals. Tumbling will probably remove part or all of the layer of plating or coating. The longer you tumble the piece the more will come off.

Gold filled wire can be tumbled for up to two hours, at your discretion. I tumble all my gold filled pieces with no problems at all and they look amazing when they come out of the tumbler.

If you aren't sure about tumbling a particular stone, or if its on the list above, be careful, some items can be tumbled briefly without mishap, but you are taking a chance that they might be damaged, especially if tumbled for a long time.

Don't overload your tumbler, you want to give your jewellery and the shot room to tumble around. It's that tumbling action that both polishes and hardens your wire jewellery.

POLISHING YOUR JEWELLERY.

Your wire jewellery creations cannot be truly called finished until you have given them their final polishing.
I believe that this is what distinguishes an amateur look from a professional jewellers finish.
If you can afford a buffing machine that's the way to go, but fear not if you can't, there are other cheaper methods that achieve very good results too.

Before we talk about those methods we need to look at polishing compounds or "rouges" as they are more commonly known.

Jeweller's Rouge Buffing Compounds

Red Rouge polishing compound

Jeweller's Rouge got its name from the jewellery industry, when jewellers would use a fine grit polishing compound to work with precious metals like silver and gold. These metals and the work pieces being of the highest quality required a polishing compound that would deliver the highest quality finish of both surface finish as well as the natural colour of the metal. Today, Jeweller's rouge refers to a specific type of polishing compound that is also designed to bring a mirror like finish to higher end metals.

Red Bright Jeweller's Rouge

The abrasive medium is a super-fine, soft red rouge combined with just enough hard grease binders to keep the compound on the buffing wheel. Used to bring out a high colour and polish on Gold, Fine silver, Sterling silver, Platinum and Brass.

White Jeweller's Rouge

An extremely dry grade of compound made with ultra-fine, soft abrasive powders. Produces a clear, brilliant, mirror-like finish on Chromium, Stainless, Carbon steel, Brass and Aluminium.

Green Jeweller's Rouge

A very dry compound made with green chromium oxide powder. Used in the jewellery trade for extremely fine colour buffing jobs on all classes of metals. To a mirror bright finish and to remove light scratch lines without disturbing the essential dimensions of the work.

Personally I have found that the RED rouge is good for most polishing jobs and gives extremely good results.

POLISHING METHODS.

HAND POLISHING.

This is the cheapest and simplest method of polishing your wire jewellery.
Simply take an old cloth (an old soft cotton T shirt is ideal) and rub red rouge on it. Rub this all over your piece of jewellery. Do not worry if it begins to turn black, this is normal.
Once you have rubbed the rouge all over, buff it all off with a clean piece of the cloth till you achieve the desired level of polish.

If you get red rouge in between wires simply take a very soft toothbrush and either some normal toothpaste or a squirt of liquid soap and clean the red rouge out of the wires, the dry with a soft dry cloth.

To keep the polish on your jewellery you can buy cloths that are impregnated with cleaners that you just give a quick rub all over your jewellery, they are called "Sunshine cloths" and are available online very cheaply.

DREMEL POLISHING.

Dremel polishing will give you very good professional results and will cost s fraction of the price of a professional buffing machine.
"Dremel" is a brand name for a multi purpose hobbyist tool that has interchangeable attachments for drilling, sanding, cutting and polishing.

There are other non branded tools available for a lower price.
You will need to use the rotary buffing pads that are about the size of a ten pence piece and usually, the wider the buffing pad, the less problem you will have with the wire getting caught up in the pad.

Apply some rouge to the pad and use it to polish your wire jewellery. Again if you get rouge between wires follow the procedure for cleaning it off with a toothbrush.

These little Dremel tools run at about 30,000 revs per minute so please be aware that the rouge will fly off in all directions and will splatter on your best curtains and newly painted walls, so best not to do this in the Lounge and keep it to the workshop/studio.

All polishing compounds will give off a lot of dust into the atmosphere so it is essential that you have good ventilation and you wear a mask when you are polishing your work.

Please remember that a light touch is needed with a dremel on gold filled wire. As it will take of the gold layer if you are too heavy handed.

Dremel tool kit

ROTARY BUFFING MACHINE

Like the dremel tool this is the same principle but on a much larger scale.
This is what a professional jeweller would use to polish their work and is the machine of my choice too. It gives an extremely high gloss and will also remove light scratches and nicks in the wire.

Apply the rouge to the one buffer wheel and apply to your piece of work.
Then move across to the second buffer wheel and polish the rouge off, till you achieve a high polish and finish. You can then finish as before with a soft toothbrush and mild

toothpaste or liquid soap to remove and residue of rouge from between wires. These machines can be bought with a housing that contains an extractor fan and filters to remove the rouge dust from the air.

I have a workbench model that sits on my bench and I use it on all my jewellery. Again you need to be careful when polishing gold filled as if you polish too long you can remove the gold finish.

Benchtop buffer and polisher

One last word of warning….please make sure you keep a firm hold on your piece of jewellery as it can be pulled out of your hand and be flung out of the back of the buffer if you are not careful. It also makes sense to use protective eyewear and a mask too if your buffer does not have an extractor fitted.

ULTRASONIC CLEANERS

Ultrasonic cleaners are useful for jewellery cleaning and removing tarnish. They use ultrasound waves and chemicals combined to create bubbles that "cling" to the foreign particles such as dirt, oil, and unknown substances. The high frequency waves are sent out and pull the contaminants off of the object. The bubbles collapse after they attach to the contaminants and move to the surface of the chemical solution creating what appears to be a boiling solution.

You can use a variety of different cleaning products in an ultrasonic cleaner, from cleaners that are organic with no chemicals to regular jewellery cleaner to diluted pine sol (for diamonds ONLY) please remember to rinse your jewellery to remove excess cleaning product, it will eliminate any soap build up left on your jewellery. Dry with a soft dry cotton cloth and buff to a nice gloss.

Ultrasonic jewellery cleaner.

The last thing to say about polishing and cleaning is that for a jewellery maker it is important that you present your work in the best light possible.
A good finish can make the difference between an amateur or a professional appearance to your wire jewellery and will certainly affect your sales.

CHAPTER SIX
PRESENTATION.

The presentation of your work when selling to the general public is important. A piece of jewellery in a nice box is going to make a statement, saying my maker values me, I am well made and I have status.
A piece of jewellery in a brown paper bag is saying my maker doesn't think much of me, I am kind of cheap really and I have no status.

When you are selling your work at shows to the general public the way you present it makes a huge difference.
In some cases if you are making jewellery from base metals and cheap components and you want to keep your profit margins small then the "pile it high sell it fast" in just a cheap bag or pouch method may work very well for you.

However if you are selling silver and gold filled jewellery and you want to realise the best price possible, then investing in good quality boxes for your jewellery makes a lot of sense.

Similarly when attending a show or craft fair the booth needs to reflect the value you place upon your jewellery and a well set out booth can increase your sales.

If you can choose your position choose a booth that is on a corner as that way you get two areas of frontage with which to tempt your public.

Putting your best pieces into a cabinet with a spotlight on it and a respectable but fair price on them will again give them a perceived higher value.

Remember to place a mirror on your booth so people can try on your jewellery. It's a fact that once a lady puts on a piece of jewellery she will usually buy it, and a mirror is an invitation to put on a piece of jewellery.

If it is possible to have lighting on your booth then some well placed spotlights will make your jewellery really sparkle.

Standing out from your competition is important and can make the difference when it comes to your sales.

FINISHING AND SIGNING YOUR JEWELLERY

When you have worked hard and acheived a good standard in your wire jewellery making it is only natural that you would want to sign your work in some way.

Because of its nature wire work can have some limitations when it comes to stamping your work with either your name or your monogram.

The narrow wires do not take readily to stamping although it is possible to get stamps made that are very small in size that you use to stamp your work yourself.

An easier way is to buy metal tags (silver or gold filled) and stamp them yourself and then attach them to your work either with wire or by hanging from a chain or catch. They are very reasonable to buy and once you have paid to have your stamp made with your name or monogram/logo you will have a way of signing/dating your work that is permanent.

Silver oval tags .   Jewellers stamp

HALLMARKING IN THE UK

A hallmark in the UK comprises of a minimum of three stamps.

The first is the fineness stamp - the number indicating the quality of metal, such as

925 for Sterling silver or 375 for 9 carat gold.

The second is the mark of the assay office which applied the hallmark. There are only four such offices in the UK - London, Edinburgh, Birmingham and Sheffield.

The Birmingham assay office has an anchor symbol as its identification mark.

The third mark is the makers or sponsor mark - usually a 2 or 3 character stamp.

There are exceptions to the law.

Silver jewellery (Sterling or fine silver) does not need to be hallmarked if the silver content of the item weighs less than 7.8 grams. For earrings this is per earring.

The same applies for gold with the weight threshold of 1 gram (and platinum is 0.5 grams). Silver jewellery under the weight limit is frequently not hallmarked - doing so is usually not economically sound, and the decision to hallmark or not is at the discretion of the maker.

As a wire jewellery maker it is not really going to affect you until you begin to make some of the larger wide band bracelets and neck collars from silver or gold wire.

You must remember that if you do make these larger items that you then sell to the public, in order to be within the law they must be hallmarked.

You should also display a hallmark certificate either on your show booth or if you have a shop, then within the sales area where it can be seen.

If you do not have them hallmarked they cannot be sold as "Silver" they must be classed as "White metal" only.

It is unlikely that the consumer protection people will enforce this law but you never know. Besides having your work hallmarked really does add to its status.

Hallmarking certificate that you display in your premises or show booth.

The most common misconception people make regarding jewellery hallmarking in the UK is that a '925' stamp for Sterling silver or a '375' or '750' stamp for 9ct and 18ct gold respectively, is a hallmark.

They are not they're simply stamps, usually added by a maker using a stamp available on the internet and while they have meaning in some countries, they have absolutely no meaning under British law.

In my experience, the vast majority of the time, these stamps are correct - i.e. the metal is what the maker claims it to be, however I've certainly come across 925 stamps applied to silver plated copper and a metal mix containing illegal amounts of nickel.

This is why, in the UK, we have strict hallmarking laws regarding jewellery.

 To legally sell jewellery that you're claiming is made of Sterling silver, fine silver or gold it *has* to have a full hallmark, applied by a British Government assay office (or an approved EU office) after metal testing.

HOW TO GO ABOUT GETTING YOUR JEWELLERY HALLMARKED.

First you must register your unique sponsor's/maker's mark so that the items that you get hallmarked can be attributed to you or your company for generations to come. A sponsor's mark comprises the initials of the person or company registering surrounded by a recognisable shield design.

Each sponsors' mark is unique.

As part of the registration process, the right size and type of sponsors' punch for your work needs to be selected.

They can be cut on two different shanks known as "straight" and "swan neck". The latter is required for marking the inside of rings but can usually also be used on other articles as well, making it the ideal choice if only one punch is to be ordered. The size of the punch is significant to the type of items to be hallmarked and choosing the correct size is paramount.

You can register your wish to have a makers mark online at all the assay office websites. Once registered and the punch has been made, your items can be submitted to the assay office to be tested and hallmarked.

HOW MUCH DOES IT COST?

The price to register your own sponsor's/maker's mark is approximately £70.00 That mark is valid for ten years and can be renewed if you wish.

The mark itself can be sized from 0.50mm for tiny items and rings right up to 6.0mm for large silver items such as trays etc.

Once you have registered at the assay office and have your maker's mark you can then send your items in to be tested and hallmarked.

The cost to then hallmark each item is approx 38p per item...plus to have your makers mark added to the hallmark is 18p per item this = approx 56p per item.

There is of course a postage and handling fee to pay as well. These details are available online at your chosen assay office website.

These postal and handling charges differ depending on the assay office you choose and how far away you are from it.

If you are within driving distance you may not have these postage charges to pay.

It may seem like a lot to payout but it is in my opinion definitely worth it for the added value your jewellery takes on.

The prestige of having your wire jewellery registered with a hallmark and your own makers mark sets it above the competition.

CHAPTER SEVEN
CONVERSION CHARTS.

WIRE GAUGE CONVERSION CHART.

Gauge USA	Diameter inches	Diameter mms
10	.1019	2.588
12	.0808	2.05
14	.0641	1.63
16	.0403	1.29
18	.0508	1.02
20	.0320	0.81
22	.0253	0.64
24	.0201	0.51
26	.0159	0.40
28	.0125	0.32
30	.0100	0.25

Recommended metal gauges (Thickness) for various applications:

It is recommended that sterling silver materials should be 10% to 25% thicker than the same materials in 14ct Gold to get comparable strength characteristics:

FOR	USA ga	EUR mm	UK ins
RINGS male	14ga	1.63mm	.0641ins
RINGS women	16ga	1,29mm	,0403ins
BEZELS	32ga		
	30ga	0.25mm	.0100ins
	28ga	0.32mm	.0125ins
EAR wires	22ga	0.64mm	.0253ins
	20ga	0.81mm	.0320ins
Bracelets	18ga	1.02mm	.0508ins
	16ga	1.29mm	.0403ins
	14ga	1.63mm	.0641ins
Reppouse	22ga	0.64mm	.0253ins

WIRE LENGTH PER OUNCE:
STERLING SILVER ROUND WIRE:

GAUGE	WIDTH	Ft/Ins Per
26	.015	75.00ft
24	.020	48.00ft
22	.025	31.00ft
21	.028	24.00ft
20	.032	19.00ft
18	.040	12.00ft
16	.051	7ft.5ins
14	.064	4ft.6ins
12	.081	3ft.0ins
10	.102	1ft.10ins
8	.128	1ft.02ins
6	.162	0ft.09ins
4	.204	5.5ins

WIRE LENGTH PER OUNCE:
STERLING SILVER HALF ROUND WIRE:

GAUGE	WIDTH	Ft/Ins Per Ounce
24	.020	96ft
22	.025	62ft
21	.028	50ft
20	.032	38ft
18	.040	24ft
16	.051	15ft
14	.064	9ft.6ins
12	.081	5.95ft
10	.102	3.75ft
8	.128	2.33ft
6	.162	1.05ft
4	.204	11ins
2	.257	7ins

WIRE LENGTH PER OUNCE:
STERLING SILVER SQUARE WIRE:

GAUGE	WIDTH	Ft/Ins Per Ounce
24	.020	36ft
22	.025	22ft
21	.028	20ft
20	.032	14ft
18	.040	9.5ft
16	.051	7.5ft
14	.064	4.6ft
12	.081	3ft
10	.102	1ft.10ins
8	.128	1ft.2ins
6	.162	9ins
4	.204	5.5ins

WIRE LENGTH PER OUNCE:
GOLD FILLED ROUND WIRE:

GAUGE	WIDTH	Ft/Ins Per Ounce
18	.040	13.96ft
20	.032	21.68ft
21	.028	28.06ft
22	.025	35.55ft
24	.020	56.33ft

WIRE LENGTH PER OUNCE:
GOLD FILLED HALF ROUND WIRE:

GAUGE	WIDTH	Ft/Ins Per Ounce
18	.040	27.91ft
20	.032	42.87ft
21	.028	59.82ft
22	.025	66.79ft
24	.020	112.66ft

WIRE LENGTH PER OUNCE:

GOLD FILLED SQUARE WIRE:

GAUGE	WIDTH	Feet Per Ounce
14	.064	
16	.051	
18	.040	10.5ft
20	.032	15.95ft
21	.028	23ft
22	.025	25.89ft
24	.020	43ft

MILLIMITRE TO INCHES CONVERSION

1 mm = approximately 1/32'	21 mm = approximately 13/16'
2 mm = approximately 1/8'	22 mm = approximately 7/8'
3 mm = approximately 1/8'	23 mm = approximately 15/16'
4 mm = approximately 3/16'	24 mm = approximately 15/16'
5 mm = approximately 3/16'	25 mm = approximately 1'
6 mm = approximately 1/4'	26 mm = approximately 1'
7 mm = approximately 1/4'	27 mm = approximately 1 1/16'
8 mm = approximately 5/16	28 mm = approximately 1 1/4'
9 mm = approximately 3/8'	29 mm = approximately 1 1/8'
10 mm = approximately 3/8'	30 mm = approximately 1 3/16'
11 mm = approximately 7/16'	31 mm = approximately 1 1/4'
12 mm = approximately 1/2'	32 mm = approximately 1 1/4'
13 mm = approximately 1/2'	33 mm = approximately 1 5/16'
14 mm = approximately 9/16'	34 mm = approximately 1 3/8'
15 mm = approximately 5/3'	35 mm = approximately 1 3/8'
16 mm = approximately 5/8'	36 mm = approximately 1 7/16'
17 mm = approximately 11/16'	37 mm = approximately 1 1/2'
18 mm = approximately 3/4'	38 mm = approximately 1 1/2'
19 mm = approximately 3/4'	39 mm = approximately 1 9/16'
20 mm = approximately 13/16'	40 mm = approximately 1 9/16'

WIRE TEMPER CHART

The better you get to know your materials the better your work will be. Using the correct gauge wire for the correct job will make a huge difference to the look and feel of your work and your customers will really appreciate your extra thought and knowledge.

Temper	Wire Sculpting	Border Wire wrap	Wrapping Wire bundles	Pin backs
Dead soft	X	-	-	-
Half hard	-	X	X	-
Spring hard	-	-	-	X

TEMPER: The temper of wire is often referred to in terms of hardness or softness. The temper or hardness of the wire indicates the malleability of the wire to hold its shape and to bend fluidly. It can range from dead soft (which bends with no resistance sort of like a wet noodle) at one end of the spectrum to extra spring hard (which is very resistant to bending) on the other.

The shape of the wire is achieved by forming the wire to the correct shape by drawing through a draw plate. The temper increases each time that the wire is drawn through the draw plate. To get dead soft wire, the wire is then fully annealed. To anneal wire is to use heat to relieve stresses in the wire, which causes a more flexible alignment of the wire molecules, thereby producing dead soft wire.

Wire temper or hardness, is often referred to by using numbers.

For example, 'one number hard' means that the wire has been drawn through a draw plate one time, and so on. Most of these operations are technical methods that only the dealers and mills perform. And, yes, you can do it all yourself with a small rolling mill, a torch and lots of muscle. But, frankly, 99.9% of all wire jewellery makers buy it already prepared and ready to go. That way you can spend more time on perfecting your craft rather than preparing your wire.

Info courtesy of Preston Reuther Master wire sculptor.

RING CONVERSION CHART.

USA	BRITISH
1/2	A
3/4	A 1/2
1	B
1 1/4	B 1/2
1 1/2	C
1 3/4	C 1/2
2	D
2 1/4	D 1/2
2 1/2	E
2 3/4	E 1/2
3	F
3 1/4	F 1/2
3 1/2	G
3 3/4	G 1/2
4	H
4 1/4	H 1/2
4 1/2	I
4 3/4	J
5	J 1/2
5 1/4	K
5 1/2	K 1/2
5 3/4	L
6	L 1/2
6 1/4	M
6 1/2	M 1/2
6 3/4	N
7	N 1/2
7 1/4	O
7 1/2	O 1/2
7 3/4	P
8	P 1/2
8 1/4	Q
8 1/2	Q 1/2
8 3/4	R
9	R 1/2
9 1/4	S
9 1/2	S 1/2
9 3/4	T
10	T 1/2

BANGLE SIZING CHART

If you would like to know how to measure bangle sizes please read below. Men's and women's bracelet sizes are given in inches, because they are open, that is they DO NOT have to be slipped over the hand as in the case of a bangle, which does not open.

BRACELET SIZES ARE GIVEN IN LENGTH OF THE BRACELET FROM END TO END.

We do not show the bangle sizes the same as the bracelet lengths because whilst two wrist sizes may be the same, the size of the hand may be different. One may have

larger hands than the other and as BANGLES have to be slipped over the hand it makes sense to take into account THE DIAMETER of the bangle that does not open. The BANGLE sizes are given in the DIAMETER which is the measurement across the inner diameter of the bangle.

DESCRIPTION		DIAMETER	LENGTH
		Inches Bangles	Inches Bracelets
Bangle/ Bracelet size	Very small	2+2/16'	6.67'
Bangle/ Bracelet size	Small	2+4/16'	7.06'
Bangle/ Bracelet size	Medium	2+6/16'	7.45'
Bangle/ Bracelet size	Medium Plus	2+8/16'	7.85'
Bangle/ Bracelet size	Large	2+10/16'	8.24'
Bangle/ Bracelet size	X Large	2+12/16'	8.63'
Men's Bangle Or Kara	Large	2+14/16'	9.02'
Men's Kara Large	X Large	3.0'	9.42'

PRONG SIZING CHART.

Prong pliers are located in the tools section of this manual.

	GEM SIZE	PRONG SIZE	PLIER WIDTH
OVAL STONES	8X6mm	19/32	2.50mm
	9X7mm	19/32	3.25mm
HIGH SET oval STONES	10X8mm	19/32	3.25mm
	10x8mm	9/16	3.25mm
	12x10mm	5/8	5.00mm
	14x10mm	5/8	4.00mm
EMERALDS			
	9x7mm	9/16	2.50mm
	10x8mm	9/16	4.00mm
	12x10mm	9/16	4.00mm
	14x10mm	9/16	4.00mm
	16x12mm	5/8	5.35mm
SMOKY	MOUNTAIN	QUARTZ	
	16x12mm	11/32	5.35mm

The prongs for the smoky mountain quartz need to be bent up at the dimples (The inside of the 180 degree turn of the prong wire)because the smokey mountain quartz has such a wide bevel on the outer table.

The prong size chart created by Ricky Jorgensen.

Type of Necklace	Average Adult size	Length and how to add for larger or smaller sizes
Bib multi stranded	12-13' and up to 20' to 23'	First strand choker length and each strand below it longer by approx 1' to 2'
Collar multi stranded	12' to 13'	Neck circumference + 1'
Choker length	14' to 16'	Neck circumference + 1.5' to 2.5'
Princess length	17' to 19'	Adjust to fit customer. Usually worn with higher necklines.
Graduated strand	17' to 19'	Largest bead in centre of necklace gradually decreasing in size towards the clasp.
Matinee length	20' to 23'	Adjusted to fit customer. Usually worn for casual daytime wear.
Eyeglass necklace	27'	Adjust to customers Preference.
Opera length	30' to 35'	Adjust to customer preference. Sometimes doubled and worn as a choker.
Rope length	40' to 45'	Adjust to fit Customer.
Lariat length	40' to 45'	No set standard. Adjust to fit the customer.

Printed in Great Britain
by Amazon

21624977R00023